MOMENTS IN GOD'S CREATION

by
April D. McCay

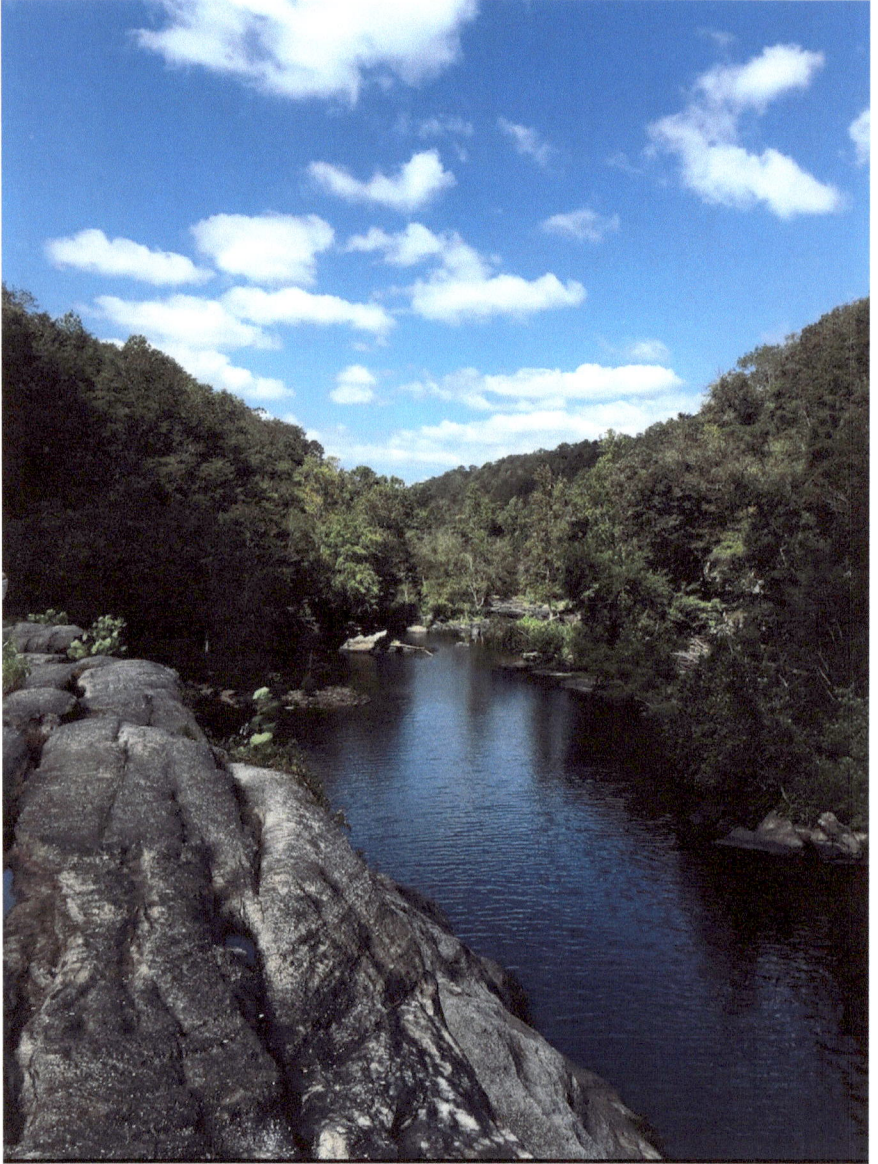

MOMENTS IN GOD'S CREATION

by April D. McCay

Southern
Arizona
Press

Southern Arizona Press
Sierra Vista, Arizona

Moments in God's Creation

By April D. McCay

First Edition

Author: April D. McCay
Editor: Paul Gilliland
Formatting: Southern Arizona Press
All Artwork: April D. McCay
All Bible Verses: American Standard Version (1901)

Published by Southern Arizona Press
Sierra Vista, Arizona 85635
www.SouthernArizonaPress.com

ISBN: 978-1-960038-36-4

Poetry

DEDICATIONS

A special thanks to my husband, Jimmy, for always encouraging me to take time to write and to my family and friends, who like him, have always believed I should try.

INTRODUCTION

This little book of poetry contains a few poetry pieces inspired by my adventures and walks outside. Just noticing the beautiful things God made. Have you ever wandered through your community and truly noticed your surroundings?

Listening...to the kids in your neighborhood play and birds singing.
Seeing...puffy clouds turn into many different creatures.
Smelling...the scent after the rain or your grandmother's freshly baked apple pie.

Explore the beautiful masterpieces God created in your little part of the world. Be inspired by the childlike nature that rushes over you as you set out to enjoy these moments, noticing the beauty in your day-to-day path.

In Matthew 13:44-46, the Bible says, *The kingdom of heaven is like unto a treasure hidden in the field ... Again, the kingdom of heaven is like unto a man that is a merchant seeking goodly pearls: and having found one pearl of great price, he went ... and bought it.* Oftentimes, we may find ourselves wandering through the routine of life instead of wondering in amazement at the people, places, and blessings right in front of us. Everything in this life has God's fingerprints all over it. Have you noticed? If not, readjust your vision.

This life is preparation for eternity. In 2 Corinthians 4:18, the Bible reads, *while we look not at the things which are seen, but at the things which are not seen: for the things which are seen are temporal; but the things which are not seen are eternal.* That verse speaks volumes! Now, what do you see?

Can you see glimpses of God in your daily commute? When we look closer, we see evidence of Him everywhere we go. Becoming almost child-like (Mark 10:13-16), we can experience all things in our path with fresh eyes once we recognize God has always been there with us. We start experiencing our family differently. *That which we have seen and heard declare we unto you also, that ye also may have fellowship with us: yea, and our fellowship is with the Father, and with his Son Jesus Christ,* 1 John 1:3. I hope you enjoy the following poetry and photographs and can see what I say!

CONTENTS

THIS VERY MOMENT

Enjoy the beauty
of your day,
notice the lovely
in your way.

This very moment
breath it in,
before it vanishes
and the memory begins.

BEFORE THE EARTH AWAKES

Before the earth awakes and the day starts,
I come to You with all my heart.

A fresh beginning waiting to be seized,
here I am, Lord, on my knees.

The day is Yours this I know,
I need your leading for the path I am to go.

Before I rise and go ahead,
let Your words upon my heart be said.

Let my ears listen deep,
for my soul is Yours forever to keep.

Give my eyes a vision from You,
let my lips speak the way You do.

Let my hands touch and care,
for I am the church in body, taking You Lord
everywhere.

THE AWAKENING OF A DAY

The sunlit hues, highlight the webs
the spiders had made,
droplets of dew now glisten
and shimmer where once was only shade.

As the fog lifts and the morning
awakens the day,
the night creatures go home
as the sun lights their way.

Morning magic in the air,
as caterpillars turn into butterflies.

But the magic does not end there
as the birds sing and the wind softly blows,
the wildflowers dance and sway to natures music
as it echoes into the valley below.

So, arise sleepy one and embrace your new day,
get up and behold the
beauty God has made.

For Jehovah will be thine everlasting light. Isaiah 60:20

CLOSER TO GOD

Is it when
in the clouds above,
one feels a closeness
of Godly love?

Soaring ever
so high,
in a plane
mesmerized by a heavenly sky.

Or could
it just be,
a walk in the woods
that inspires a prayerful knee?

Breathing in
God's fresh air,
is this like Adam's walk in the garden
as he walked with God there?

Oh how
can my heart look like Thee?
A closeness
I desire, everlasting eternally.

No matter the place
my heart finds You there,
closer to God
a destination to share.

It's an inward location
now I see,
closer to You, O Lord,
is where I want to be.

Whether surrounded
by clouds or by trees,
I want to search for You Lord
in my heart and on my knees.

IN MY FOLK'S GARDEN

In my folk's garden
of course, you will find,
an area of serenity
and flowers of many kinds.

A place where the birds
have their own bath,
moss laden pebbles
bordering a path.

Future butterflies
finding their wings,
buzzing of bees
pollinating all the pretty things.

A lizard and frog
scurrying and hopping around,
a peaceful place
where Jesus is found.

A place you can listen
and He will whisper in the wind,
it may not be Eden but a lovely place to walk
with Jesus, my friend.

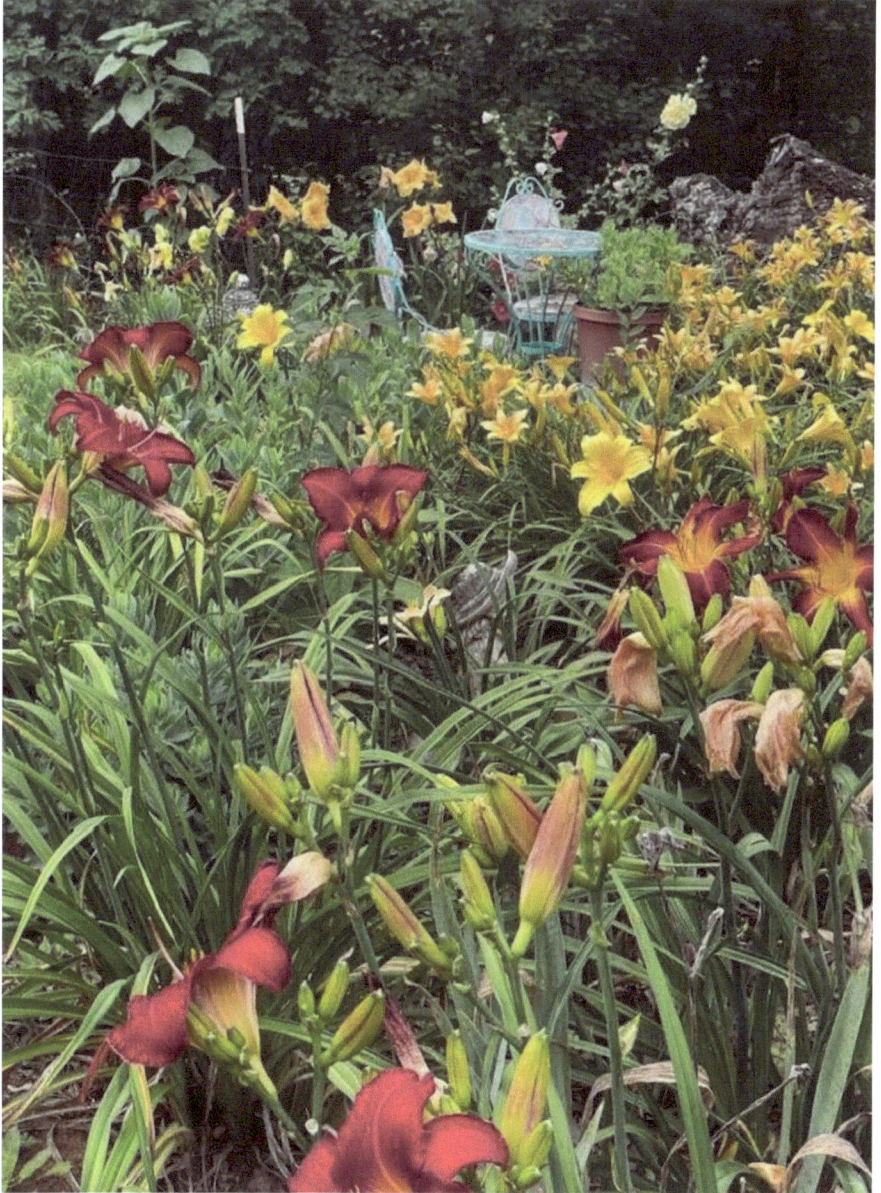

THE GOLDEN LEAF

I search the forest deep,
in aim of finding the golden leaf.
Many trees boast limbs with leaves of green and
    red,
my search continues on a road of pine cones, I
    now tread.

The sun offers a shimmering light,
the season of fall is now within my sight.
The magic of autumn displaying a colorful show,
bursting forth with warm hues and cool breezes
    that seem to follow.

The breeze shuffles through my hair,
I catch a glimpse of golden, spiraling from
    midair.
The golden leaf . . . Could it be?
I journey closer, for I must see!

I ran pass a deer, disappearing into the forest
    deep,
the excitement of the season causes my body to
    leap.
I skip along the trail in search of the golden leaf,
listening to pine cones as they crunch beneath
    my feet.

The red cardinal leads the way,
as I ponder the path God has me on today.
He created this all, including the leaf I seek,
I raise my hand and twirl, as I listen to my
    Creator through nature speak.

I give God praise and blindly dance into a field of
    gold,
I open my eyes, oh the many golden leaves my
    eyes behold!
The golden leaf is not the only treasure I found,
I found God always with me, in a field where
    golden glitter abounds!

THE BREEZE OF FALL

The breeze of fall
awakens my senses,
and my imagination runs wild.

The true beauty of the season
stirs something within me,
my most favorite season of them all.

God's chilly breath of wind
I notice rustling the leaves in the air,
as He decorates in warm hues, the trees so tall.

The smells of chili, soups, and fire,
bringing seasonal comfort as a flannel blanket to
    you all.

THE REVEALING OF SPRING

As the sun arises
the ground begins to weep,
morning dew trickles down
blades of grass, rooted deep.

The warmth overtakes
the chill of cold,
a spectacular landscape
creatures behold.

The fog lifts
revealing the season of spring,
trees branches budding
while birds loudly sing.

Butterflies dance
curious deer pause and stare,
a powder of pollen
now sprinkles the air.

The heavens declare the glory of God;
And the firmament showeth his handiwork.
Psalm 19:1

April D. McCay

THE WILDERNESS OF FINER THINGS

*But blessed are your eyes, for they see; and your ears,
for they hear. Matthew 13:16*

The stars are my diamonds
the ocean is my wine,
the birds are my orchestra
outside, my thief of time.

The mountains are my distant castles
the wilderness is mine to explore,
in the streams are my glass slippers
awed and childlike, I step into God's lovely world.

The wind is the rhythm
to which I dance,
and audience of trees
captures my glance.

I discover a pearl in a field
a priceless journey, my heart sings,
out of the wilderness
into the promised land of finer things.

*Read Matthew 13:44-46

BEFORE THE DEADLINE

Dazed before my deadline
as my pen taps my head,
words waiting to be written
or as I like to call it . . . the invisible dread.

Pushing my laptop aside
my feet meet the floor,
my hand grips the door
exiting outside to explore.

Imagination now igniting
senses are engaged,
the colors, the smells, the sounds
I rush back to my last page.

There's something about distraction
that welcomes fresh words,
it's like a mental muscle memory
revealing a gift to be heard.

All is coming together now
minutes before I submit,
one last look over
now, the return key I hit.

ABOUT THE AUTHOR

April D. McCay lives in the Roll Tide state and is an author of poetry, devotional articles and human-interest stories that have been published in *The Blount Countian* and the *Cullman Tribune* and you will find a few of those included in this publication. She has won awards from Southern Christian Writers Conference for her poetry and newspaper articles of hope and inspiration. Last year her short story and essay article was published by the group. Her hope is to one day publish a fiction novel, well, maybe five or more, Lord willing. She has also created journals using her photographs which are available on Amazon. On most days, she can be found outside looking for inspiration with her camera phone in hand, taking pictures and writing notes for a future article or poem. She enjoys pancakes (Kodiak Cakes, so it is a health food, right?) for breakfast and looks forward to spending time with her husband outdoors.

www.ingramcontent.com/pod-product-compliance
Lightning Source LLC
Chambersburg PA
CBHW041810040426
42449CB00001B/47